Praise for Daniela Gioseffi

"Visionary and powerful with tremendous vitality . . . Daniela Gioseffi is a gifted, graceful and moving writer." — GALWAY KINNELL

"Everything Daniela  things, I'd put my life in her hands." — (

D0873566

"A vital international au ....ated to planetary survival."
— CECILIA CERIANI, EL PAIS, MADRID

"One of the finest new poets around, and I feel ashamed that I was not aware of her work until now. It overflows with poetic vision, but nothing is ever pretentious or done for effect. She has achieved what the surrealists hoped for poetry."
— NONA BALAKIAN, FORMER STAFF REVIEWER OF THE NEW YORK TIMES.

"It's been a pleasure to spend time with Daniela Gioseffi's books; her work is brilliant, compassionate, and timely."
— D. NURKSE, FORMER POET LAUREATE OF BROOKLYN

"Gioseffi's writing is irresistible, engaging, filled with energy, and appealing good humor. The pace never slackens . . . ."
— LARRY MCMURTRY, THE WASHINGTON POST

"Wake up! It's truth time, brought to you by Daniela Gioseffi."
— BOB HOLMAN, PRODUCER OF THE UNITED STATES OF POETRY FOR PBS TELEVISION

Waging Beauty

Also by Daniela Gioseffi

Pioneering Italian American Culture: Escaping La Vita Cucina
with Angelina Oberdan (editor)
New York: Via Folios / Bordighera Press, 2013.

The Story of Emily Dickinson's Master, Wild Nights! Wild Nights!
New York: BookBaby, 2013.

Blood Autumn / Autunno di sangue: Poems New and Selected
with English to Italian translations by Elisa Biagini, Luigi Bonaffini,
   Ned Condini, Luigi Fontanella, and Irene Marchegiani.
Boca Raton, Florida: Via Folios / Bordighera Press, 2006.

*Women on War: An International Anthology of Writings from Antiquity to the
   Present*
Editor
New York: The Feminist Press at the City University of New York, 2003.

Symbiosis
New York: Rattapallax, 2002.

Going On: Poems
Lafayette, Indiana: Via Folios / Bordighera Press, 2001.

In Bed With the Exotic Enemy: Stories and Novella
Greensboro, North Carolina: Avisson Press, 1997.

Word Wounds and Water Flowers: Poems
West Lafayette, Indiana: Via Folio / Bordighera Press, 1995.

Dust Disappears: Poems of Carilda Oliver Labra
Translator, with forward by Gregory Rabassa
Merrick, New York: Cross Cultural Communications, Inc., 1995.

Wildlife of Northwest New Jersey: An Introductory Guide to the Birds,
Mammals, Reptiles and Amphibians of the Skylands Region
with Pamela Mading
Andover, New Jersey: Ladybug Publications, 1994.

On Prejudice: A Global Perspective
Editor and introduction
New York: Anchor Books / Doubleday, 1993.

Women on War: Essential Voices for the Nuclear Age from a Brilliant
International Assembly
Editor, with illustrations by Kathe Kollwitz
New York: Simon & Schuster, 1988.

Earth Dancing, Mother Nature's Oldest Rite
Harrisburg, Pennsylvania: Stackpole Books, 1980.

Eggs in the Lake: Poems
with foreword by John Logan
Brockport, New York: BOA Editions, 1979.

The Great American Belly Dance
Garden City, New York: Doubleday 1977.

A Brooklyn Bridge Poetry Walk
Editor
Brooklyn, New York: Print Center, 1972.

I listen to the voice of the cricket,

loud in the quiet night,
warning me not
to mistake a hill
for a mountain

Daniela Gioseffi

Verse Etched in Marble. Seventh Avenue Concourse, Penn Station, New York City

Waging Beauty

As the Polar Bear Dreams of Ice

Daniela Gioseffi

POETS WEAR PRADA • Hoboken, New Jersey

Waging Beauty: As the Polar Bear Dreams of Ice

Copyright © 2017 Daniela Gioseffi

All rights reserved. Except for use in any review or for educational purposes, the reproduction or utilization of this work in whole or in part in any form by electronic, mechanical or other means, now known or hereafter invented, including xerography, photocopying and recording, or in any informational or retrieval system, is forbidden without the written permission of the publisher:

Poets Wear Prada
533 Bloomfield Street, Second Floor
Hoboken, New Jersey 07030
http://pwpbooks.blogspot.com

First North American Publication 2017
First Mass Market Paperback Edition 2017

See Acknowledgments for a list of prior publications.

Special thanks to Ms. D'Alessio for granting permission to use her photo for the cover of this book. The original photo appeared on her husband Jon D'Alessio's blog *Where Are They Now?: Travels with Jon & Catherine.*

ISBN-13: 978-0997981155   ISBN-10: 0997981156

Library of Congress Control Number: 2017937568

Printed in the U.S.A.

Front Cover Photo: Catherine Dobbins D'Alessio, *Iceflow,* Iceland, 2015
Author Photo: Anton Evangelista, 2014
Frontispiece Photo: Anton Evangelista, 2014

Dedicated to my beloved talented daughter, Thea,
and my bright and creative grand sons, Ellery and Keir,
and to the future of children everywhere.

I understand the tree, it does not reason . . .
Fawns you have had your day:
the poet now wants to talk to the tree.
— Jules Renard

Table of Contents

Foreword

The Romantic Movement in art and literature did us the considerable favor of restoring deep emotion to poetry. But, unfortunately, every gain carries loss on its back: another legacy of that movement is the continuing notion that poets are and must be forever young, irresponsible, and more than a little eccentric — preferable crazy.

This notion, so contrary to the facts of literary history, which constantly reminds us of the existence of the great and mature — and perfectly sane — writers in the Western canon, persists despite a plethora of what the scientists call "negative instances." It persists in the minds of some poets and critics apparently because it conforms to a prevailing esthetic: poetry must be 99% inspiration, 1% perspiration.

So nobody criticizes Villon for being an outlaw rogue, or Chatterton for being crazy, or Byron for being a reckless rascal, or Baudelaire for being *maudit*, or Lowell for being mentally disturbed, or Plath for being suicidal, or any of the currently fashionable poets who claim to be writing *about nothing* and writing so abstractly as to convince us that they are indeed writing about absolutely nothing. But let a poet, serious about her art and craft, speak solemn poetic truth about the world we live in, and she can expect to be pilloried for her honesty and for her engagement with so called *politics*—as if politics can be separate from life and meaningful art, when, especially in our time, politics determines if we have clean water to drink, clean air to breathe, or a future for the children on our planet.

Enter Daniela Gioseffi, who for years has been giving the lie to those, now. venerable clichés of our trade. Not only by her own poetry, but also, in her tireless activism for poetry and justice, she has shown us the importance of being both earnest and engaged. Her substantial and award-winning output and her anthologies of world literature, *Women on War: An International Anthology of Writings from Antiquity to the Present* and *On Prejudice: A Global Perspective* are impressive displays, of both prose and poetry by artists, around the world and throughout history, deeply and passionately involved in social justice, ideological, and, yes, *political* themes.

In this new collection, Daniela Gioseffi's poetry continues to be concerned, compassionate, and justifiably angry at times, but it is also imaginative, lyrical, personal, and loving. Anyone wishing to stereotype her work would have their job cut out for them. She makes a driving and headlong assault on the heartlessness of our corporate society. She exudes a properly indignant feminism in "Cataclysmic Carousel of Greed," where she takes on the voice of a mythic Cassandra who tries to give warning, driven insane by those who do not listen to her alarm. In "Let the Gold Go Free," the poet assails the greed that despoils our Earth, the poisonous avarice for gold which must be "set free" so that "luscious apples" can bloom to feed our bodies and lift us from despair — greed that's destroying children's futures and all civilization with it.

Here is a poet aware of how the destructive elements in our lives may be overcome by our personal attachments, our commitments to the beauty that is truth. In *Waging Beauty*, it's the beauty of truth and the salvation of the natural world she bids us to wage instead of war and the ruination of our earthly resources. Her sympathy and empathy are everywhere in her poems, throughout her many books, and in this new collection where she displays her never-ending love for nature and the intricate and mysterious science of which it and we are composed in our interconnected ecosystems. She makes poetry of photosynthesis and atmospheric balance with respect for biological truths in an unfathomable universe, reminding us we are made of the very dust of exploding stars. There is humor, too, in poems like "Big Hearted, Witty, and Wide Eyed" or "Where Have All the Flowers Gone?"

This is a book for Humanists, for those who think that this world is worth the saving, this life worth living — and worth learning to live in better than we have. Especially in the title poem that laments, "News of atrocity travels at the speed of light. / Emotional reservoirs grow shallow with horror after horror. / . . . / Drone attacks in flashing pixels / dull our senses. Fanatics send wounded cries rising / from Earth's surface," yet later continues, "There's a blueprint to butterfly cocoons / stored in genetic memories, / as there's an art to growing dreams in the young."

Characteristically, after all despair is realized, this Humanist poet, who believes in the glories and natural sciences of the world, bids you to "Grip your spirit like a hand grenade! Let the world see / how resiliently fierce, gorgeous, and dangerous / a militant sunflower can be. Wage beauty / as the polar bear dreams of ice!" She reminds us that it all comes down to personal responsibilities in a world of collective communities where lives influence each other and "we all breathe the same atmosphere of breath."

Anyone, who still thinks that a poet cannot write about important, serious, and contemporary subjects without the burden of false rhetoric, should take a lesson from this book. Daniela Gioseffi gives us loving lessons in conscience and art from science and imagination.

Philip Appleman

Waging Beauty

Some Slippery Afternoon

A silver watch you've worn for years
is suddenly gone, leaving a pale
white stripe blazing on your wrist.

A calendar, marked with appointments
you meant to keep, disappears, leaving
a faded spot on the wall where it hung.

You search the house, yard, trash cans
for weeks, but never find it.

One night the glass in your windows
vanishes, leaving you sitting in a gust of wind.

You think how a leg is suddenly lost
beneath a subway train, or taxi's wheel,
some slippery afternoon.

The child you've raised for years,
combing each lock, tailoring each smile,
each tear, each valuable thought,

suddenly changes to a harlequin,
joins the circus passing in the street,
never to be seen again.

One morning you wash your face,
look into the mirror, find the water
has eroded your features, worn them

smooth as a rock in a brook.
A blank oval peers back at you,
too mouthless to cry out.

Carbon Summer or Nuclear Winter?

"Some say the world will end in fire. / Some say in ice."
— *"Fire and Ice" by Robert Frost*

I look in my grandchild's eyes,
watch his small hands spin his toy globe
as Earth's fever rises. Glacial cliffs slide
into rising seas. Cities drown in flooding ports.
Climate refugees migrate upland to alien cultures
where religions clash in wars. Storms batter cities.
Forests cleared for greed rip species from the web of life.
Everyday millions of tons of brain-damaging poison
are dumped into the delicate shell of Earth's air
as if it's an endless sewer up there.
Reservoirs dry, cities burn in thirst.
Faltering farmers lose their living.
Pollinating bats, honeybees, butterflies and hummingbirds
die weakened by herbicides and pesticides.
Amphibians and birds diminish to extinction.
People of the Arctic and Pacific islands flee ancient lands.
Wildfires foul air and force thousands from burning homes.
Nuclear radiation spreads by tsunamis and earthquakes
as wars topple governments. Weapons dealers profit
as tanks and bombers guzzle oil.
Where lies collide with eco-logic,
battlefields bloom with blood.

I watch my grandson's small hands spin
his toy globe, and realize there could be
no eyes, no ears, no hands, no art, no song,
as our dusty planet, home to our dried tears
of love and laughter — lost in endless space,
could rotate frozen or burning in silent thirst.

Some say the world will end in carbon summer,

Some say in nuclear winter —
but from what I've seen of carbon fire,
nuclear winter's ice is also great
and would suffice.

Waging Beauty As the Polar Bear Dreams of Ice

"Though we travel the world over to find the beautiful, we must carry it
with us or we find it not." — Ralph Waldo Emerson

Innovative imagination can save hummingbirds
as the polar bear dreams of ice, but we wake
to news of dictators' slaughters of babies,
hungry people's haunting swoons. Bloody faces,
swollen bellies fill our nightmares with weeping tunes
of grieving mothers, massacred fathers,
school children riddled with bullets.

News of atrocity travels at the speed of light.
Emotional reservoirs grow shallow with horror after horror.
Automatic guns sold everywhere to anyone,
filthy fossil fuels causing famines, floods,
tornadoes, tsunamis, hurricanes, nuclear accidents,
melting glaciers. Drone attacks in flashing pixels
dull our senses. Fanatics send wounded cries rising
from Earth's surface as people are chopped in pieces
to praise Allah; crucified to satisfy Jesus; threatened
with vengeance by Jehovah; children are starved,
abused, made to soldier weapons, or are raped by priests.

There's a blueprint to butterfly cocoons
stored in genetic memories, as there's an art to growing
dreams anew in the young. Dancers show feeling;
singers share emotion; scientists fulfill hope —
or horror, even as warring gods can be expelled
from patriarchal thrones to stop us waging wars,
instead of waging beauty, in their mythic names.

We stand on graves of those who built pathways before us.
Our dreams are in the genes of our children. Will those
who visit our graves, keep or scatter our ashes,
name our time "The Age of Murdered Imaginations?"

Will they groan about what we didn't do:
clean geothermal, solar, wind energy left unused,
while their bodies were wounded by pollutants,
as their dreams turned to oil slime,
their hopes become coal dust,
as gas drills poison their waters?
Will our apathy be defined as shell shock from witnessing
the destruction of everything we loved, until our psyches
were numbed? Will graves become more attractive to
our children than city streets;
sad defeat their only emotion?

Revolution without purpose is evolution with amnesia.
Real revolution reclaims resources, rallies peace.
Can we envision ourselves in a healed world,
on a glowing green globe of swirling blue waters?
Can we fall deeply in love with dreaming an Earth renewed?
"We are such stuff as dreams are made on."

We can dance, paint, compose an eco-philosophy.
We can make compassion more desirable than numbness.
Nature and imagination are our truest gods.
People driven by affirmation have emotional power.
They don't burn out. It's so much easier to criticize than love,
but those who harbor visions of love wage beauty over war.

Our American empire's a blink in the eye of creation.
We've been told that gravity is real and dreams are not.
We believe we deserve bruises, beatings, and abuse —
in the streets and from the state. What would we do
if gravity was an illusion and oceans fell off the earth?
Would rain clouds float to other galaxies?
Can flowers sing to their seeds while birds listen enraptured?
Will we last longer than dinosaurs?
What should we exhale into our delicately

thin veil of atmosphere?
What would the Earth be without atmospheric
balance or without photosynthesis?
What could the Earth be like the day after
the last prison and insane asylum have closed?

Grip your spirit like a hand grenade! Let the world see
how resiliently fierce, gorgeous, and dangerous
a militant sunflower can be. Wage beauty
as the polar bear dreams of ice!

Vases of Wombs

For the Venus of Willendorf

For a long time,
I've thought about this body of mine
with agony, curiosity, and dreams
of caressing lovers and children.

I've thought about these arms as if they
belonged to an Etruscan priestess, raising
them over her head to pray or protect hunters;
or as handles on the hips of an ancient
Greek vase standing in the still light of a museum.
I've listened to blood flowing through these arms
and crossed them over my breasts to imagine rest.

I've thought about these buttocks,
how they've held me to the Earth while others fly
and inhabit high shelves of libraries.
I've thought about these peering nipples,
feelers on a cat's face, sensitive to night.

Men accept mead, soma, nectar from my hands;
blood from my womb, fish from my eyes,
crystals from my eardrums, food from my glands.
In return, they try to pierce the heart
that ticks between my thighs,
pinning me to the bed like a butterfly.

These arms fly out of themselves to talk to you.
This head becomes small and sightless.
These breasts and buttocks swell
until they're all that's left of me, until
flooded Earth is melted
and Her gardens are wildfires.

Earth Is Feminine in Most Languages: An Essential Libretto for a New Age Symphony

After a passage in the Mundaka Upanishad

From food comes all, all that lives upon the Earth.
All is food, and to food all shall return.
Food is goddess among the living.

They are blessed with food, those who worship Earth,
for the Earth is food and goddess among the living.
All are born of food, and by food all grow.
All eat Earth, and She eats all.
Food we are,
and to food we shall return.

That is why She is called Sugar! Blossom! Honey!

In the beginning the Great Mother gave milk.
She arose as a dream from mud.
From Her comes food; and from food, breath, spirit,
    truth, worlds, and in works immortality.

What is the role of the poet now that Earth is suffocating —
carbon rising, glaciers melting, rivers drying; libraries
drowning — books drenched by tidal waves, tornadoes, hurricanes;
farmlands dried with droughts or drenched in mud?
Who needs music, poetry, art on a dying planet home?

What climate refugee will read while thirsty or starving?
Many have lived without art, love, or electricity,
but none without food, air, water.

In the beginning the Great Mother gave milk.
She arose as a dream from mud.
From Her comes food; and from food, breath, spirit,
    truth, worlds, and in works immortality.

Where Have All the Flowers Gone

For Pete Seeger and Joe Hickerson

They've been poisoned everyone by
PCB's, Hollywood silicone-pumped bodies, fake news,
plutonium, Larry Flint's porn, Strontium 90,
weedkiller, paint thinner, carbon fluorides, Coca Cola
saccharine, aspartame, glyphosate from Monsanto,
BGH & BST, hormones in cows' milk, nitrites in meat,
causing breast, colon cancers, and leukemia in children.
Cocaine, crack, steroids, painkillers! Greed
and Neo-Goth grunge; mega-stressed,
smart-ass, abstract and abstracted poets;
funky religion, occult bullshit, fake torn bluejeans,
dumb smart phones, pie in the sky, pill in the gill,
faecal matter in the orange juice of the O.J. blitz,
sports opiate, baseball scores of the World Serious,
leaders fiddling away while Rome burns
like an over-baked pizza of roadkill
on the sidewalks of New York, Tokyo, Paris and
London where the Queen
pretends she never smelled a fart
with her funky style, handbag all a twiddle
with treacle — nose high — while her kids
sexed their brains out, wasting fortunes
and the people! Ah, the people —
they that dwell up in the steeple
wait to be beheaded by gilded silver teapots,
or hatchet blades, by a lack of air, and drinkable water!
Oh yeah, global warming is here with skin cancer
everywhere, while people of conscience —
drowned out by Hollywood and Twitter tweets —
feel smart jokes are all there's time to deal out
this year, when everything, everything falls with

the bright leaves through a dark
hole in outer space, sucked into disappear.

"The roll call will find everything
six feet under the rising sea,"
said the bee to the honeysuckle
as he buzzed his last high,
and shouted "UP YOURS!"
to the hot over-heating sky.

When will we ever learn?*
When will we eh-eh-eh-ever learn?
When will we ever,
ever, ever, ever,
ever learn? When will we —
flowers gone — when? *Where have all*
the young girls — young boys —
gone?†
In uniform,
everyone?

When
will we —
shall we, can we —
overcome‡?

---

* "Oh, when will we ever learn?" is the refrain of the American folk-style protest song "Where Have All the Flowers Gone?," original version (melody and the first three verses) written by Pete Seeger in 1955 and released in July 1960 on *The Rainbow Quest* album (Folkways LP FA 2454). Seeger's song was updated with additional verses in May of 1960 by Joe Hickerson.

† The words "where have all the young girls gone" opens and is repeated in the second verse of "Where Have All the Flowers Gone?" by Pete Seeger and Joe Hickerson.

‡ "We Shall Overcome" is a traditional gospel song which became a protest song and a key anthem of the African-American Civil Rights Movement in the Sixties.

Let the Gold Go Free

"All that glisters is not gold." — *Shakespeare,* The Merchant of Venice

Let it be free! Let it flow
over mountains and coat trees.

Let it out of the cities.
Release if from the safes and banks.
Let it run from the vaults like a glimmering river.

It shouldn't be kept for a few women's necks
or a few men's wrists.

It's fear of the absence of oranges and wheat
that keeps the gold a prisoner from the streets.
It's songs about ashes and birds kept in cages.
It's clothes, hiding bodies from faces,
that keeps the gold in heat.

It's the nutritious golden dandelion
not allowed to seed,
murdered with tons of weed killers,
so fertilized lawns
can poison waters with nitrates.

Let the gold go free.
Let it pour over me, melted.
Bake it in a pie!
Chew it with fury!

It's the garden, wandering homeless,
in the midst of lawns and cities.
It's apple trees, discriminated against,
banned from our neighborhoods,
that could be here, wearing luscious apples,
giving us what we've come to Earth to eat.

13

Earth's Body in True Genesis

Meteorites and comets delivered carbons from outer space
to Her smoldering surface. Carbons full of amino acids seeded her —
proteins of life from dust of stars in balls of ice smashed into Her:
some big as mountains; others small as pebbles, exploded as they slammed
into Her smoldering mass, creating *peptides.*

The leap to life began in deep sulfuric caverns where bacteria blossomed
with nuclei, sucking energy from subsurfaces where heavens of microbes
flourished, living on exotic diets of gases, methane, sulfur . . .

DNA erupted from oceans where chemicals inside Her forming soil
spewed into warm waters, feeding to bloom life as a half-billion years ago,
meteorites and comets stopped their Big Bang bombardment. She cooled
as immense colonies of green slime fed by the sun and photosynthesis
began, spreading vegetation over the cooling surface of Her mass
still spinning from the first huge explosion.

Forests formed up and down peaks and valleys of Her early beginnings.

In the hills of oceans of *stromatolites* where sticky cells of bacteria migrated
to tops of rocks to live as microbes and drink sun, cities of tiny bacteria
lived reaching up out of Her shallow waters, breathing out oxygen
combining with iron in the Age of Rust. Layers of oxide built streams
of iron ore on the floor of Her primordial oceans.

Cyanobacteria, blue-green algae breathed out oxygen, filling Her
atmosphere, overpowering noxious gases so living creatures could endure. A
layer of ozone ascended as a veil over Her. Then came fish, reptiles, insects,
birds, primates, finally, humans in the last few "moments." Now, here we are
in all our complexity, murdering each other over an unborn god. All art,
music, poetry, religions have not stopped wars as Her glaciers,
air-conditioners for Her life, melt in the sun, deflected from a carbon doom
of man-made pollutants, causing Her oceans to rise. One day,

when humans have stopped wasting energy on bloody weaponry, they'll turn
and look into their children's eyes and be inspired — seeing newborns
as the only true angels. And maybe then, they'd let God — who is actually
compassion — be born. Then the angels, made of stardust,
made of carbon, hydrogen, oxygen, would build new homes
in the universe where other life blooms to befriend.

Maybe then, God might finally exist — as Earth's body.

Imagine all the pounding hearts . . .

  pumping billions of gallons of blood,
lakes of tears, echoes of laughter!
Imagine more than seven billion
human lives throbbing;
and the rhythms inside rocks,
rhythms of atoms spinning,
planets circling in space,
clocks ticking, rhythms of tides
obeying the moon; worlds turning
in trillions of universes expanding,
spinning with their burning stars exploding,
and here on our small planet, Earth,
our rock home full of molten gasses,
people killing each other over their gods.

A grandmother combs the hair of a child.
Her hands move in rhythms of water
running over stones and pebbles,
flowing like love to thirsty mouths.

The creosote on fence posts beneath the Earth
keeps them standing, but wood finally rots
as worms chew in the rhythm of clouds
floating across skies, changing shapes,
viewed like Rorschach tests by those
who look up dreaming into endless blue.
There are secrets hidden in throats of caves,
crying screams in waterfalls, rustling leaves,
stirrings underground, the dead reborn as grass.

All wondered by each feeling life among the billions as one
merges into another, as a hand with an opposing thumb
picks up a book and reads of the time of galaxies,

crustaceans, primates. Our Earth began four point five billion years ago, but we, humans, arriving merely two hundred thousand years ago, now destroy our habitat — Earth and all her sentient beings pumping billions of gallons of blood.

Dinosaurs, Comets, and Consumers

After reading cosmologist Lisa Randall

Sixty-six million years ago, a tiny twitch caused
by an invisible cosmic force hurled a comet
three times the breadth of Manhattan
toward Earth at 700 times the speed of a freeway car.

The collision stirred the strongest earthquake known,
released energy a billion times that of an atom bomb,
heating the atmosphere to an incandescent furnace,
killing three-quarters of Earthly life. No creature bigger
than fifty pounds survived. Death of the dinosaurs
gave mammals dominance. So, we've evolved
to ponder perplexities of the cosmos.

Extinctions destroy life, but reset conditions
for evolution. From dinosaurs evolved birds
that sing to us mornings, animating our skies.

Meteorites deposited amino acids that became seeds
of our lives. Parallel truths give complex richness in grand
schemes more wondrous than we imagine. The deadly comet
that birthed us mammals took light years to reach Earth
and quake dinosaurs to extinction. Their fate was sealed
in a cosmic blink when dark matter jolted the icy comet
out of orbit. Rilke said: "The future enters into us . . .
to transform itself in us long before it happens."

Gestations of consequences can be immensely long:
We've been heating our breathable atmosphere, a thin
veil around our planet home, for two hundred years.
In our lifetime the human population doubled, straining Earth's
resources, changing cosmic events billions of years in the making.

Our impact on Earth is a fast-moving comet headed for doom with

only a short time left to avert its deadly course, a catastrophe
we've aimed at ourselves with contagious consuming.

Testimony Before Dying

I'm the youngest one left at seventy-six,
Yesterday, I was nineteen, a journalist intern in Selma
on WSLA-TV — first to integrate Deep South TV
Now all my friends are dying, one by one;
I'm waiting my turn, and it's no fun.

Today, the Commander-in-Chief gave money
to war widows. Some ripped it up. Some
ate it and wept, drying their tears on folded flags,
Others jumped out of the window with it.
The presidents and politicians said,
"I'm sorry. That's how war is."

I stuff my ears with music,
fill my breast with song to drown out
the din of bombs falling on Syria, Yemen,
as the USA sells billions of dollars of weapons
to Saudi Arabia, a murderous monarchy,
paid for by our taxes. Photos of
wounded babies stab my old gut the most,
make me turn the happy music up
to drown out cries of small voices,
after I send my contributions to
Save the Children or UNICEF,
wishing they could be enough.

Historians say, "War seemed necessary.
Oil wars ruled the twentieth century."

Now black gold has tainted air,
made history its usual horrifying bloodbath.
Today, Daesh beheaded a twelve-
year-old boy, a boy the same age as my
grandson, a child without will, killed for

over trumped-up war gods. Who will win
the final war? Will the dug-up skulls talk
and confess? Will there even be anyone left,
after the sixth mass extinction's climate chaos,
to dig them up and ask them who won?

Chant for Sioux Water Protectors at Standing Rock

"Many have lived without love, but none without water." — W.H. Auden

Oil is ancient fossilized death
  putrefied life rotting for centuries
    deep in the bowels of Earth.
Water is life. Oil is death.

Death was drilled from bowels of Earth,
  spilled in oceans
    to foul water and kill
      sea life on which we live.
Water is life. Oil is death.

Death was pumped from Earth's underground
  and spewed into our children's breath
    as asthma and lung disease.
Water is life. Oil is death.

"Black gold" was pulled from Earth's guts
  and dumped into skies as climate chaos:
    super storms, earthquakes,
      droughts, wildfires, floods.
Water is life. Oil is death.

A world powered by living Earth
  can now be built
    under shining sun
      and stirring wind.
Water is life. Oil is death.

If political will is not strangled by greed,
  strangled to death, strangled to death,
    it could be done. It can be done!
*Water is life returned by the sun
  driven by wind, driven by wind.*

Hands, Mouths, Fire

For the children of Aleppo

When fire falls from heaven,
I cover my eyes with my hands
and beg forgiveness for greed,
thievery, killing, and for my rapist's sin.

When fire has fallen from the sky,
I hide amidst tallest rubble rocks,
crouch low, cover my head with my hands,
lament my fate, pray for redemption.

When fire falls from heaven, I dig among ruins
with bruised hands for buried children,
take them in bleeding hands, hold them, caress them,
kiss their crying mouths, comfort those who live,
and with aching hands bury, bury,

bury the dead so that vultures can't sail them
heavenward for you, patriarchal God of War.
You don't deserve the children's bones
scattered on your bloody carpet —
in your golden-throne room.

O God of War, of greed, jealousy,
envious thief of joy, murderer of Mother Gaia,
grinning with children's bitten flesh
hanging from your mocking mouth,
century upon century.

Cataclysmic Carousel of Greed

"Turning and turning in the widening gyre. / The falcon cannot
hear the falconer; / Things fall apart; the centre cannot hold."
— William Butler Yeats, "The Second Coming"

A cataclysmic carousel of greed
turns the world, spinning death high on the wing,
turning faster and faster in *widening gyre.*

Cassandra rides weeping, yelling warnings
for the spinning children who ride with her,
rotating on Earth's breast, our only home
where our young will die of droughts,
thirst, floods, and hunger.

The children ride behind her, crying,
"No more killing our Mother Earth
with war and drilling!" Earth erupts,
quaking from all the drilling.
Seismic blasting in the Arctic seas
deafens whales and dolphins, killing
them and us. "No more drilling!"

Earth's glaciers melt, oceans warm gaining weight,'
shifting Her tectonic plates. Tsunamis surge
from acid seas, washing tons of fish ashore,
as Cassandra weeps her dirge with Yeats:
. . . *what rough beast, its hour come round at last,*
Slouches towards Bethlehem to be born?

Cassandra goes insane, crying, yelling:
"No more drilling, no more killing!" The Trojan Horse
is galloping with mad falconer astride
shouting his slogans, leading his army.

Cassandra, weakening, spins warnings

on a cataclysmic carousel, whimpering:
"No more drilling! No more killing!"

Now's the Time

Now's the time to save all
as we all breathe Mother Gaia's breath
Now's the Anthropocene Age,
a time of human threat to Gaia's breath,
when we've become our own judge of
whether life's worth our children living.

Now's the time when human progress can be
inhumane. Father Sun impregnates Mother Earth
while Daughter Moon tugs making our planet
the only one in our system with an elliptical
orbit that offers temperate zones
for lively possibilities.

Now's the time to see dark energy as the brain
of God, threaded with strings of light,
vibrating with music of the spheres,
reminding us we are made of stardust.

Now's the time for us to know God is the music
of the Universe, and strings of light
in God's mind vibrate with our lives. Hate and love
are forms of energy from the breast
of a milk-giving mother. All is melody
and mystery and ours now to conduct.

Now's the time to know we all breathe
one atmosphere of breath, and life is not all vanity
and greed but worth living.

Across the World I Feel the Others Awakening

After reading Kathleen Dean Moore of Oregon who watches the
marsh hawks fly while I watch the trees sway against streetlamps
in the city

How can I sleep? So much work to be done to save children, to save birds,
elephants, whales, books bears, food fields from flooding, farms from
drought, children from hunger, thirst and painful, slow dying. We could
work all the bright day and all through the dark night, and still our work
would not be done. I lay awake in a darkened room, holding one hand with
the other, feeling my small being in the vast night, feeling my spirit inside my
head, trying to keep itself calm with deep breathing. Who sleeps well when
the whole world of everything we love and all art everywhere needs saving?

There's no love without life, no faith without children to leave it to. As day
darkens I watch bare branches slice the falling sun as if it were a ruined
sunflower. As we fall into bed despondent, because we have not yet saved the
world, the sun rises on the other side of the planet where people awaken to
protect what food still flourishes, what drinking water still flows, what's
simply beautiful to view. On the rotating Earth, there's a chorus of dawn, of
committed people, millions of them trying to save the uncommitted and
innocent children who rise from their beds or mats or blankets to sip coffee
or tea, and begin the work of defending the poor and the thriving. We can
hear the chorus if we listen — the rustle, the creak of metal, wood, or grass
doors. Voices call to each other in a thousand languages! Roars of action
begin around the world, as we awaken like birds to our rising sun to fly and
search, sing and try.

When night comes will I sleep, thinking of the work of others, exhausted,
lying down all over the world to rejuvenate for the work ahead. There's a
song in the cradle of dawn. Sunset and sunrise on different sides of the
rotating Earth, home to all. Each of us emerges from sleep, from our dark
shelter of dreams and nightmares, from our private despair. We find our
cause, our chorus, our courage. Nothing can stop our collective will to save
everything for the children, for the libraries full of wonder, for the sunsets
and rises to come — not Trump's troopers, not Big Banksters, sniveling

oligarchs, complacent professors, passionless preachers, crony politicians, fake news reporters or those who think there's more important causes than saving all life and art.

Nothing can distract us — not sports, not shopping, not praying, not composting. There was a time when our work for the world was in private lives, recycling, not eating forest-destroying, methane-producing meat. That time's passed! Private work's good but not enough. Now, the work is in streets, in state houses, on the riverbanks, on college campuses, in churches, and green sanctuaries, on paths by the flooded fields or drought-stricken farms. What we cannot do alone, we can do only together. This is not the end of my small story but our big beginning to save everything from extinction forever. Forever!

The Plan

God is the love all of nature creates in us,
and greed for things is killing this beautiful life.
— *Donato Gioseffi (1905 —1981), philosopher, Puglia, Italia*

The plan was for butterflies,
bees, and bats to suck among flowers,
gathering sweetness to live
as they carried pollen, seed to ova
to bring fruit from need.

The plan was for waters
to run freshly through
wetland deltas, filtering streams
along their way from mountain tops,
quenching thirst, running clear —
rivers to the sea — bringing life to the lips of children,
blossoming from the need for love,
from parents — two different creatures united
by a new being, ecstatic with rebirth.

The plan was for forests to clean the air
for children's breaths, in symbiotic balance,
using carbon dioxide expelled from animals
to give forth oxygen
to photosynthesize food, from need,
making green leaves that leaf and leaf again,
to feed women's breasts — not mere objects of sex —
but factories of milk, first link
in a food chain for children's mouths
to suckle, milk from leaves of grass
arising from fertile mud sown by need.

But sheer greed for things of plastic,
polymers from petroleum —
acrylic, polyester; germ warfare,

29

nuclear radiation, nitrites — poisons;
greed for too much meat full of steroids
laid land to waste by grazing cattle,
carcinogens, plutonium, filth and waste.

Greed killed the plan slowly, bit
by bit, until the water trickled
with foul waste of industry mistakes
and what was needed — food, water, breath —
was suffocated to a barren death.
Bats, bees, and butterflies
ceased to buzz around flowers
bearing no fruit from their sexual union,
so animals had no food.

Forests, chopped to dust,
gave forth no oxygen, photosynthesis,
or atmospheric balance
as fuel emissions, creating a dusty dome
of polluted atmosphere,
trapped sunlight and melted Earth
to muddy doom, leading to
a Sixth Extinction wherein
Love, emanating from Gaia Herself,
no longer breathed
within the eyes of children
but was silenced from song;
and art, books, poems,
had no feelings to speak
as all seed,
through market engineering,
was lost to greed.

Mother Gaia

She's our largest living being.
We've seen Her from outer space,
one big blooming woman. We're all born out of Her
sapphire globe, gleaming with frothy white waves
and the browns and greens of forest and farm.
We saw Her from outer space, and life recognized life.

She emerged flying from the sun's explosion,
spun Herself into roundness so to rotate
endlessly, journeying round the sun. Primal being
without mouth, legs, arms, anus, genitalia,
she sails round the sun, spinning us through days
into sleep-filled nights. Her moon creates tides on Her
watery surface. Hospitable regions of Her lands and seas birthed
many organisms and, finally, the ones with consciousness:
we who issued from Her, we individuals of Her global community, we —
all of us — Her children. We, dependent upon Her atmospheric balance
and photosynthesis fostering multitudinous varieties
                    of consumable vegetation.
Spewing lava, molten glass from sand, burning, acrid, smoking,
Gaia, it seemed, had no future. Who would have thought
that from Her roundness so many beings would be born?
Who could have guessed that from Her flaming hot magma
forests, cities, songs, art, poetry, longings would be born?

Please come be Her celebrant with me,
hope with me that our children, born of Her womb, will live
with Her breath, breathing with Her trees in symbiotic balance,
bathing in Her cleansed waters, tranquilly together.

Earthlings suckled by Her full-breasted bounty
                    of brown-gray earth and blue-green waters —
Mother Gaia, our only teardrop of love and laughter,
                    afloat in cold dark space.

Big Hearted, Witty, and Wide Eyed

Earth! She's been around for about 4.5 billion years.
And the first third of Her billions were mayhem.
Meteorites crashed in to Her. Magma everywhere!
Acid rain falling on Her until finally
Her first wildlife, fungi, started forming.
Then only single-celled ocean critters
for another third of those billions of years.
Sex life didn't show up until the last third
of those billions of years — in the Cambrian Age —
plant-animals with weird fronds
and sea tubes copulating like seahorses.
Trilobites paddled around for a few billion years
more until ancient forests grew, and dinosaurs
crunched among Her trees,
chewing Her photosynthesizing leaves.

We humans have been here a very short time.
Before us came mushrooms, fish, orangutans, chimps, and
Neanderthals. And with us humans —arrowheads,
Cleopatra, fireworks, guns, and the naming of stars.
And you and I, with our mp3s and books,
our masquerade costumes and fancy shoes,
regrets, dreams, hopes, mouths we've kissed —
or wished we'd kissed, have existed for a
microscopic bit of time, a slice of time so comparatively
thin you'd need a microscope to see it.
Just take a file off that bit of time and you'd wipe out
Shakespeare, ancient Greece, Dante and the Bible,
to say nothing of all those hundreds of Hollywood flicks.

We're each a mote, dancing in a beam of light
for a second that's passing amid crowds of over seven billion
alive today, and billions dying yesterday? So I say

be big hearted, witty, and wide eyed with wonder!
Read about the Anthropocene Age, love some others,
paint, sing, taste everything lawfully possible,
and help save the kids from Climate Crisis,
because you still have some hours left.

Beyond the East Gate

I listen to the voice of the cricket,
loud in the quiet night,
warning me
not to mistake a hill for a mountain.

I need to be alone,
in a private house with doors that open only outward,
safe from strangers who smell of death,
where I can draft a universe under my eyelids
and let nothing invade it.

I want to sing a fugue,
sounding like the genius of flowers
talking to leaves on their stems,
to have more concrete meaning
than even the dance of a child in my uterus.
I'm a lost and primitive priestess
wandering in a walled city of the wrong century.
I need to spend thirty years in the desert
before I will understand the sun,
thirty years at sea
to gather the blessing of salt and water.

In the back room of my skull
a secret dice game determines
the rites of my hands
before they touch flesh again.
I want to reach a peace I've never known,
to be an old woman who's very young,
a child who's a sage,
come down from the mountain.

I hope Earth will remember me —

that ashes of my spirit, my words,
my love will live in new life fertilized by me.

I hope I'll nurture the roots of a tree,
feeling singing birds on its branches.

I'd love to be heard in the song of a river
as it flows through green mossy forests.

I'm glad all the water I drank will be recycled
for flowers to drink in new gardens I'll never see
except in my dream of coming spring.

Snow falls in my sleep now
as I long for cricket sounds — night's comforting
music. I hope my aging, calcified bones
will nurture strength in children to be.

I long for an Earth of tomorrows,
where new beings might recall
the good things we're made of,
born of — exploding stars— in this mysterious
life of sorrow, beauty, longing, and love.

Dancing Song for My Daughter

Stars dance their light.
Night sky shivers.
Listening to waves,
dance, my daughter!

Wind wanders fields,
singing in wheat.
Hearing wind songs,
dance, my daughter!

Earth spinning holds
children in her skirts.
Feeling the moon's hands,
dance, my daughter!

Love, winning, fills
all with her power.
Seeing her sunrise,
dance, my daughter!

Love, losing, sighs
in wet wounded eyes.
Burying my bones, smile
and dance, dance,
dance, my daughter!

Acknowledgments

The author would like to thank each publisher and editor of the various publications where some of these poems previously appeared, sometimes in a slightly different format or version.

"Some Slippery Afternoon" *Cries of the Spirit*. Ed. Marilyn Sewell. Boston: Beacon Press, 1991.

"Carbon-Summer or Nuclear Winter?" Robert Frost Foundation Facebook page, posted May 8, 2015, with a link to a recording of the 2015 Honorable Mention awarded poem by the author, archived on Sound Cloud.

"Waging Beauty as the Polar Bear Dreams of Ice" *Forfattenes Klimaaksjon: Norwegian Writers' Climate Campaign*, January 26, 2014.

"Vases of Wombs" *Eggs in the Lake: Poems*. Brockport, New York: BOA Editions, 1979,

"Earth Is Feminine In Most Languages" *Ms.* Magazine, July1978.

"Where Have All the Flowers Gone" *Going On: Poems*, Lafayette, Indiana: Via Folios / Bordighera Press, 2001.

"Earth in True Genesis" *Estrellas en el Fuego (Stars In the Fire)*. New York: ANDYSWIPE Anthology Series / Rogue Scholars Press, 2014.

"Imagine all the pounding heart . . ."   *Forever Night (Siempre Noche).*
New York: ANDYSWIPE Anthology
Series / Rogue Scholars Press, 2017.

"Dinosaurs, Comets, and Consumers"   *Eco-Poetry,* March 2017.

"The Plan"   *Going On: Poems,* Lafayette, Indiana:
Via Folios / Bordighera Press,2001;
Reprinted in *The New Verse News,*
November 2013.

"Mother Gaia"   *Eco-Poetry,* 2015; *Author and
Activist: The Daniela Gioseffi Story,* a
film by Anton Evangelista, 2016.

"Big Hearted, Witty, and Wide Eyed"   *Persimmon Tree: Literary Journal,*
December 2016.

"Beyond the East Gate"   *The Nation,* October 5, 1974, p. 316.
Reprinted in *Eggs in the Lake:
Poems,* Brockport, New York: BOA
Editions, 1979.

"I hope Earth will remember me —"   *Eco-Poetry,* March 2017.

"Dancing Song for My Daughter"   *Word Wounds and Water Flowers,*
West Lafayette, Indiana: Via Folio /
Bordighera Press, 1995. Reprinted
with Italian translation in *Blood
Autumn,* Boca Raton, Florida: Via
Folios / Bordighera Press, 2006.

About the Author

Daniela Gioseffi, an American Book Award-winning author, has had seven volumes of poetry, including a translation of the work of Cuban poet Carilda Oliver Labra, two novels, and a collection of stories published by major presses. She is also editor of the online anthology *Eco-Poetry: Climate Crisis Literature* and five print anthologies including two compendiums of world literature *Women on War: An International Anthology of Writings from Antiquity to the Present* and *On Prejudice: A Global Perspective,* both earning Gioseffi Ploughshares World Peace Foundation grant awards. Both books were presented at the United Nations. Her sixth book of poetry, *Blood Autumn: Autunno di sangue,* earned her the John Ciardi Award for Lifetime Achievement in Poetry in 2007. Gioseffi has also garnered the OSIA NYS Literary Award and two grant awards from the NYS Council of the Arts.

Eco-Poetry is a international anthology of climate literature, founded by Gioseffi in 2010, receiving over 5,000 global visitors monthly. The anthology includes works by Ernesto Cardenal, Galway Kinnell, Alicia Ostriker, Al Gore, and Marilyn Nelson, among many others.

A documentary film of Gioseffi's life, *Author and Activist,* telling her story as a young white female journalist who integrated Deep South television (Selma: WSLA-TV, 1961), the resulting sexual abuse by the KKK, and of her continued activism — in the anti-nuclear, women's rights, and climate justice movements — was produced and directed by the prize-winning filmmaker Anton Evangelista. The film previewed at the Maya Deren Theatre in Manhattan in September 2014 and has been screened throughout the Metropolitan area, at various campus theaters — Hofstra University, St. John's University, The Calandra Institute at CUNY, St. Francis College — and at the Unitarian-Universalist Women's Retreat on Long Island, among various other places.

Gioseffi has performed her poetry on NPR, BBC, the Library of Congress radio show *The Poet and the Poem,* and at the Geraldine Dodge Festival and Poets House, NY. In 2002 the first verse of Gioseffi's poem "Beyond the East Gate" was etched in marble on a wall of the Seventh Avenue Concourse at Penn Station, where it still remains, alongside verses by Walt Whitman, William Carlos Williams, and Amiri Baraka.

About the Cover Photographer

Award-winning wildlife photographer Catherine Dobbins D'Alessio is a retired American doctor. She and her husband, the attorney Jon D'Alessio, retired at the end of 2008 and now the pair spend much of their time traveling around the world with their cameras. This is their new "job." Their photography focuses on wildlife, and they are especially interested in animal behavior. Jon maintains a blog of their travels and photographs, *Where Are They Now?: Travels with Jon & Catherine*. Here you can find the stories of their adventures as they try to capture the wonders of nature and get that perfect photograph.

Their unique photographs have garnered Catherine and Jon several individual prestigious awards. Most recently, two of Catherine's bird photographs, "Arctic Tern" and "Atlantic Puffin," received Audubon photography awards in the Amateur Category and were listed among Audubon Magazine 2016 Photo Awards Top 100. Previously three of her photographs, "European Bee-Eater," "Brown Pelican" (also selected photo of the day for June 09, 2014 by Todd Petty) and "Adelie Penguin" were included in Audubon Magazine 2013 Photo Awards Top 100. Also in 2013, Catherine's "California Quail Caught by a Spring Breeze While Standing on a Fence Rail at Point Reyes" was selected by the San Francisco Bay Bird Observatory as that year's Click Off People's Choice winner in the Bird Portrait Category, appearing in the SFBBO publication *Bay Bird Review*. Jon's photograph of a Herring Gull taking off in Norway was selected by Audubon as one of their Top 100 photos of 2015.

The D'Alessios recently returned from a tour of Italy after visiting Northern Greece to photograph the Dalmatian Pelicans, the largest pelicans in the world, on Lake Kerkin. Next on the agenda for 2017 are excursions to Namibia and Newfoundland before setting out to photograph the Canadian Polar Bears.

A NOTE ON THE TYPE

This book is set in Minion Pro, an Old-Style serif typeface designed by Robert Slimbach of Adobe Systems, and released in 1990 by Linotype. Inspired by the mass-produced publications of the late Renaissance, but with a contemporary crispness and clarity not possible with the print machinery of that era, even by the best of the Renaissance typographers, this modern-day interpretation is well regarded for its classic baroque-rooted styling and its enhanced legibility. One of the five or six most widely used typefaces for trade paperback fiction published in the United States over the past several years, Minion Pro is the typeface adopted by the Smithsonian for its logo. The name Minion is derived from the traditional classification and nomenclature of typeface sizes; *minion*, the size between *brevier* and *nonpareil*, approximates a modern 7-point lettering size